MW00768707

108 WAYS TO CREATE HOLISTIC SPACES

 *feng shui and green design for healing and organic homes*

ANJIE CHO

Copyright © 2015 Anjie Cho

All rights reserved.

ISBN: 1502995646

ISBN-13: 978-1502995643

Library of Congress Control Number: 2015900613

Anjie Cho, New York, New York

No part of this book may be reproduced or transmitted in any form or by any means, electronic or mechanical, including photocopying, recording, or by any information storage and retrieval system, without written permission from the author.

For information address Anjie Cho, info@anjiecho.com

Book design by Chippy (Heung-Heung Chin)

DEDICATION

*T*HIS BOOK IS DEDICATED TO MY MOTHER AND FATHER.

Thank you for creating safe, loving,

and nurturing spaces for me throughout my entire life.

CONTENTS

ACKNOWLEDGMENTS

I WOULD LIKE TO THANK MY TEACHERS,
WHO HAVE MADE THIS BOOK POSSIBLE:
the late His Holiness Master Lin Yun,
Rosalie Prinzivalli, Barry Gordon,
and especially Steven Post for his many hours
reading and advising me on the manuscript.

Thank you also for teaching me that I am a treasure,
the jewel in the lotus. *Om Mani Padme Hum.*

FOREWORD

by Steven Post

Geomancy/Feng Shui Education Association
Author of *The Modern Book of Feng Shui*

ANJIE CHO'S *108 WAYS TO CREATE HOLISTIC SPACES: FENG SHUI AND GREEN DESIGN FOR HEALING AND ORGANIC HOMES* SHOWS A NEW DIRECTION IN PROVIDING SIMPLE HELP TO IMPLEMENT THE BENEFITS AND BLESSINGS OF FENG SHUI AND GREEN DESIGN. If you follow her suggestions, you will create spaces in your home and workplace that support your dreams and advance your life.

When I was a child in the 1960s, feng shui was virtually unknown in the West. Even in China, many rejected this profound art and science as superstition. As the first person to teach and consult in feng shui in the West (even before my master, His Holiness Professor Thomas Lin Yun, Da Shih, a living Buddha, came to the United States and opened the roads for feng shui to be an international force), I have seen interest grow from a trickle to a torrent. My childhood dream of understanding and using the unity of person, place, and universe to help mankind has become a reality. Professor Lin Yun asked me and two colleagues to create a professional education program to train skilled practitioners to benefit society. This three-year program, of which my friend and student, the eminent architect Anjie Cho, is a graduate, continues as the BTB Feng Shui Masters Training Program in New York City in partnership with the New York Open Center. It is the only program of its type to have state accreditation.

Of my many students, Anjie Cho is one of the most gifted. In the six years that I have known her, she has earned my respect as a student able to bring feng shui knowledge into accord with modern architectural practice and green design to advance her ideal of holistic feng shui.

I knew that Anjie's book would be of high quality and relevance even before she asked me to read the text, make suggestions, and write this foreword.

I have witnessed her interest, application, long-term study, respect for the tradition, ongoing commitment to self-improvement and gaining knowledge, and kindness and wish to help the world. Each of these is an important characteristic of a good feng shui consultant. Anjie has attended many consultations with me both as a student and after she graduated the masters program. She has provided excellent analysis and suggestions for residences, businesses, and localities, drawing upon her broad studies in architecture and green design and on the feng shui knowledge that she shares so cogently in this book.

In the first part of her book, Anjie presents key concepts and applications of the feng shui bagua map, also known as the ever-changing eight trigrams. In an easy-to-understand format, she provides many concepts, techniques, and tools for transforming and improving environments, including how to use colors most effectively. She draws upon her knowledge of the method of minor additions, selecting the easiest and most effective ways of applying light, life, color, five element theory, and more in a way that is truly easy to integrate with how people now live and work. She includes secrets of the "commanding position," and describes the power of intention to allow you to position yourself for success and to bring both visible and invisible forces to support your life. She also includes simple and effective methods of space clearing to cleanse and invigorate your home or office.

In the second part of the book, Anjie shares how to create an inviting entry to receive what the world brings to you. She also conveys how to create a lively and entertaining living room to support life's pleasures and comforts. She imparts how to create a kitchen that will nourish you at many levels, including contributing to your advancement in the world, and conveys how your dining room can best support satisfaction in eating and also connect family members and friends. She explains how to skillfully set up a home office, co-coordinating practical aspects of feng shui and green design. She shares bathroom basics and techniques for both protecting your wealth and making your bathroom friendly to the environment. She also offers good advice and best practices to make your bedroom a fortress of comfort and repose. Her discussion of this important influence on our lives includes examining how to select the right bed and what you need to know to make your bedroom nurturing, supportive, and encouraging of a wish-fulfilling life.

Anjie also discusses where best to meditate, the meaning and best use of closets, the role of plants, and how to understand and employ doors and windows, the mouth and eyes of your home, including how to correct some difficult door and window situations so that what once may have created a life problem is transformed into an uplifting and supportive environmental factor.

108 Ways to Create Holistic Spaces: Feng Shui and Green Design for Healing and Organic Homes concludes with a section on how nine minutes a day of feng shui maintenance, support, and activity can help you easily move toward your goals.

Let Anjie take you by the hand and lead you on a path of learning and self-improvement in correctly and creatively adjusting your environment. I encourage those who open this book to read it thoroughly, think about what is presented, and implement the suggestions. You will bring the blessings of holistic feng shui and green design into true effectiveness. Starting with yourself, advance on this true path toward a better life for yourself and the world.

1
INTRODUCTION

"*Your sacred space is where you can find yourself over and over again.*"

—JOSEPH CAMPBELL

WHAT ARE HOLISTIC SPACES? Holistic spaces are designed by looking beyond the surface to create awareness and an environment that supports and nurtures the inhabitants. Holistic design seeks to create spaces that resonate from both the inside and the outside— from your spirit, your body, your home, the planet, and the universe as a whole.

In creating holistic spaces, I combine many different disciplines, including feng shui, green design, and environmental psychology.

I like to say that feng shui is the original "green design." Through observing and shifting the built environment, feng shui teaches us how to live in harmony with nature. Eco-friendly design looks at your own personal health and also how human actions impact nature and the earth. Feng shui looks at the same issues: how does the environment affect us on an energetic level and, in turn, how do we influence the planet as a whole?

Feng shui is an ancient Asian art of placement developed thousands of years ago. Feng shui seeks to enhance and improve the flow of energy through your environment, to maximize the positive potential for your life. A truly holistic way to look at your environment, it may include interior or architectural design, but it's really more than that. Feng shui looks beyond the superficial and is about creating awareness beyond what you see on the surface. The intent is to create an environment that nourishes you holistically.

Feng shui adjustments can bring balance to your home because the principles are founded upon cycles and patterns of nature and ancient knowledge. Sadly, many of us have lost touch with this knowledge. Feng shui can teach us to be in tune with our environment and aware of how we impact the earth, as well as how it affects us.

I primarily practice BTB feng shui, which is one of the many schools of feng shui. I find that BTB feng shui is more relevant for me and my clients as westerners, because it focuses on intention to empower the adjustments and the flow of qi rather than a compass direction. I feel this is more compatible for us because we are not living in ancient China. Therefore, most of the suggestions in this book are based on the BTB feng shui philosophy.

As a holistic interior architect, I encounter many people who wish to integrate feng shui and eco-friendly design into their homes and businesses, but they want to wait until the space is clean, or until they have more time, or until they move. These are, of course, appropriate times to renovate or redecorate, but what most people don't know is that you can incorporate feng shui and green-living principles at any time. It may even be more helpful at a challenging time. This is about more than just moving furniture around; it's about shifting your environment physically and energetically to support and nurture your life. Even if you are not ready to renovate or redesign your home, you can still incorporate holistic principles into your space.

Feng shui can be simple and straightforward. Take some time and look at how you can rearrange your lifestyle and position yourself in command of your present to encourage relaxation and allow the best of you to shine through. Recognize that you are actively making a small change to let the universe know you are ready to accept the best things that are coming to you.

Getting Started

YOU CAN USE THIS BOOK AS A REFERENCE GUIDE, OR SIMPLY READ ONE OF THE TIPS EACH DAY. Remember that this is not about seeing dramatic results. Instead it is about amassing small shifts and noticing the subtle changes that happen. Please take time and delight in the simple shifts in your environment as well as your perceptions. Feng shui and green lifestyle changes can influence mindfulness in all aspects of your life.

Remember, this is just the tip of the iceberg when it comes to creating holistic spaces. I'm sharing simple and effective tools to help you begin to make shifts on an environmental level. To truly take the holistic approach, open up your awareness. I encourage you to go beyond your space and make personal, social, universal transformations.

My aspiration is that each of my readers begins to make some shifts to create harmonious living and work spaces to support and nurture healthy and conscious lives.

THE
FENG SHUI
BAGUA MAP

"True happiness is always available to us,

but first we have to create

the environment for it to flourish."

—SAKYONG MIPHAM

The Feng Shui | BAGUA Map

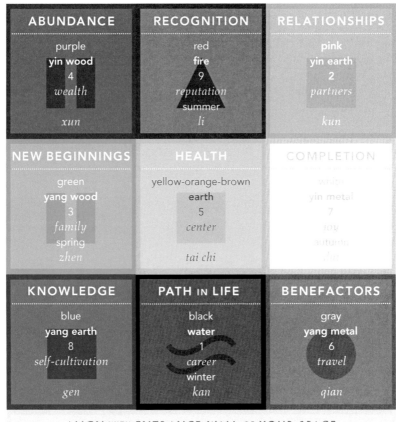

ABUNDANCE	RECOGNITION	RELATIONSHIPS
purple	red	pink
yin wood	**fire**	**yin earth**
4	9	2
wealth	*reputation*	*partners*
	summer	
xun	*li*	*kun*

NEW BEGINNINGS	HEALTH	COMPLETION
green	yellow-orange-brown	white
yang wood	**earth**	yin metal
3	5	7
family	*center*	*joy*
spring		autumn
zhen	*tai chi*	*dui*

KNOWLEDGE	PATH IN LIFE	BENEFACTORS
blue	black	gray
yang earth	**water**	**yang metal**
8	1	6
self-cultivation	*career*	*travel*
	winter	
gen	*kan*	*qian*

ALIGN WITH ENTRANCE WALL OF YOUR SPACE

HOLISTIC  SPACES

How to Lay the Bagua

1

TO USE THE FENG SHUI BAGUA MAP TO THE LEFT, PLEASE ALIGN THE BOTTOM OF THE MAP WITH THE ENTRANCE WALL OF YOUR SPACE (THE WALL THAT CONTAINS YOUR DOOR). Stand in the doorway of your home, office or any room and face into the space. Divide the room in a 3x3 grid. You will be standing in the Knowledge, Path in Life, or Benefactors area. The Abundance area is in the far back left corner, and the Relationships area is in the far back right corner.

The bagua is one of the most important aspects of feng shui, as it assists in determining which parts of your space relate to each specific type of energy. Without defining this correctly, you cannot properly execute feng shui. Look into which bagua area relates to an area that you need to work on, and get started!

Note: This is my simplified version of the Feng Shui Bagua Map. Each of these areas can expand to relate to every aspect of your life. You may feel the urge to correct them all, but please remember not to make this about perfection. My teachers taught me to only work on the areas that need attention. Be kind to yourself and choose the three or so areas that you can truly and honestly work on with your best effort.

New Beginnings

2

Where We Always Begin

IN FENG SHUI WE OFTEN START WITH THE NEW BEGIN-NINGS AREA OF THE BAGUA OF THE HOME, **ZHEN**, WHICH IS RELATED TO NEW BEGINNINGS OF ANY KIND— CREATION, FAMILY MATTERS, AND THE SEASON AND ENERGY OF SPRING—AND IS SYMBOLIZED BY THE COLOR GREEN, THE NUMBER THREE, COLUMNAR AND TALL SHAPES, AND THE ELEMENT OF YANG WOOD. It has that magnificent burst of energy associated with a sprout pushing out of the ground and the excitement of the first beautifully sunny and warm day of spring.

This is a great area to work with if you have trouble starting new things. You may also choose to activate this area if you need support in new projects or more harmony in your family.

As the first way to create holistic space, please take some time and place something meaningful in this area to symbolize a new start to creating a healing and organic home. A green plant or water fountain may be especially effective in this area to inspire growth and the nourishment that you need to heal.

Abundance

Overflowing Fullness

THE ABUNDANCE AREA OF THE FENG SHUI BAGUA, CALLED **XUN**, IS RELATED TO WEALTH, ABUNDANCE, PROSPERITY, AND SELF-WORTH, REPRESENTED BY THE COLOR PURPLE, THE NUMBER FOUR, COLUMNAR AND TALL SHAPES, AND THE ELEMENT OF YIN WOOD. Yin wood energy is like a big tree grounded with deep roots and a large canopy.

This is one of the most popular areas of the bagua. It is not just about money, though. Your wealth in the world is dependent on and related to your self-worth, so this area is also about having an abundance of the positive aspects in your life.

What is going on in the Abundance areas of your home, particularly in your bedroom and office? Take some time and place something meaningful in these areas of your bedroom and/or office. If you need some stability in your finances, try a heavy statue. If you need more cash flow, a water fountain may be especially effective in this area.

Health

4

The Center of Your Home

THE HEALTH AREA OF THE FENG SHUI BAGUA IS CALLED *TAI QI*, WHICH IS RELATED TO YOUR OVERALL HEALTH, SIGNIFIED BY EARTHY COLORS (YELLOW-ORANGE-BROWN), THE NUMBER FIVE, SQUARE OR FLAT SHAPES, AND THE ELEMENT OF EARTH. If you look at the location of this area, it is in the center. The energy of the center affects physical, mental, and emotional health.

The health area is in the center because it affects and is influenced by all eight bagua areas around it. This central area touches all aspects of your life, so of course it influences your health and well-being.

A great way to support your overall health is to activate the tai qi of your home. A yellow-toned square rug in the center of your bedroom, living room, or home provides centralized stability and helps to create interconnectedness with people and the various aspects of your life.

Benefactors

Assistance from the Heavens

THE BENEFACTORS AREA OF THE FENG SHUI BAGUA IS CALLED **QIAN**, WHICH IS RELATED TO HELPFUL PEOPLE, BENEFACTORS, THE ENERGY OF HEAVEN, TRAVEL, AND THE FATHER, ALL SYMBOLIZED BY THE COLOR GRAY, THE NUMBER SIX, CIRCULAR SHAPES, AND THE ELEMENT OF YANG METAL, LIKE UNREFINED METAL ORE WITHIN THE EARTH'S CORE OR A SWORD.

Oftentimes we need help from others, whether that be people or the heavens, to move forward. Adjustments can be made in this area to bring supportive energy and people into your life.

If you need some support, place a metal wind chime in this area of your home. When the chimes ring, the sound will let the world know that you need support. You can also try a large piece of pyrite or labradorite in this area. Pyrite brings in more fatherly energy and protection, giving you support. Labradorite attracts heavenly energy to connect you to the universe. These crystals from the earth support the metal element of the Benefactors area.

Completion

Children of All Kinds

THE COMPLETION AREA OF THE FENG SHUI BAGUA IS CALLED *DUI*, WHICH IS RELATED TO COMPLETION, CHILDREN, ANY SORT OF OUTPUT OR OFFSPRING, JOY, AND THE SEASON AND ENERGY OF AUTUMN. The color white, the number seven, circular shapes, and the element of yin metal, like delicate and polished shiny jewelry, relate to Completion.

Completion is about closure and the end of things. But ends bring new beginnings. This area would be great to activate if you have trouble completing projects.

This area is also about joy. A great way to bring joy into your life is to keep fresh flowers in the completion areas of your bedroom, living room and entry. The fragrance of flowers is transformative and brings life energy into your space. Fresh flowers are also excellent at "un-sticking" things that are "stuck." Get that joy and qi flowing!

Knowledge

Self-Knowledge and Cultivation

THE KNOWLEDGE AREA OF THE FENG SHUI BAGUA IS CALLED *GEN*, WHICH IS RELATED TO KNOWLEDGE AND SELF-CULTIVATION AND IS REPRESENTED BY THE COLOR DARK BLUE, THE NUMBER EIGHT, SQUARE AND FLAT SHAPES, AND THE ELEMENT OF YANG EARTH, LIKE A BIG MOUNTAIN YOU MIGHT CLIMB TO MEDITATE AT THE APEX.

This area is about your spiritual inclination to grow and develop your inner life. It's also about your level of skill and wisdom in mundane areas of your life such as your career.

The Knowledge area is a great place for your library, books, and/or a meditation space. Reading books can educate you and help to improve your proficiency and skillfulness in all areas of your life. Similarly, meditation assists in your spiritual development. These activities may be doubly effective if done with clear intention in your Knowledge area.

Anjie CHO

Recognition

Fame and Passion

THE RECOGNITION AREA OF THE FENG SHUI BAGUA IS CALLED *LI*, WHICH IS RELATED TO FAME, PASSION, RECOGNITION, REPUTATION, AND THE SEASON AND ENERGY OF SUMMER. The color red, the number nine, triangular shapes, and the element of fire symbolize the Recognition area.

Pay attention to this area if you want to be seen and recognized. It influences and improves your level of passion and how the world sees you. It is a great area to activate if you are starting any new endeavors that require public support.

If you need more recognition in your life, at work or in your relationships, try placing a plant in this area of your desk (for work) or bedroom (for relationships). The wood of the plant will feed and cultivate the fire of Recognition.

Path in Life

The Steps You Take

THE PATH IN LIFE AREA OF THE FENG SHUI BAGUA IS CALLED **KAN**, WHICH IS RELATED TO YOUR CAREER AS WELL AS THE SEASON AND ENERGY OF WINTER. The color black, the number one, wavy shapes, and the element of water symbolize this area.

This is the path you walk in life, and how you express your efforts in the world. It does not necessarily have to be a traditional career, but it pertains to how you move through the course of your life.

If you need some more support in your career you could do some adjustments in this area of your home or office. A water fountain with the flow of water directed toward the center of the space is ideal. This will also encourage cash flow for the inhabitants if placed near the entry of the home.

Kun

10

Relationships

THE RELATIONSHIPS AREA OF THE FENG SHUI BAGUA IS CALLED **KUN**, WHICH IS RELATED TO RELATIONSHIPS, PARTNERSHIPS, THE MOTHER, AND MARRIAGE, AND SYMBOLIZED BY THE COLOR PINK, THE NUMBER TWO, SQUARE AND FLAT SHAPES, AND THE ELEMENT OF YIN EARTH, LIKE SAND ON A BEACH.

This area is probably the second most popular because it can activate attracting a primary relationship. But relationships can also refer to business partnerships or other important connections in your life.

If you are looking to attract a romantic partner, this is the area to work on. It is best to work on the Relationships area in your bedroom, which represents you and also your future partner. One powerful adjustment is to select two pieces of tumbled rose quartz and place them in the Relationships area of your bedroom. If you already have a partner, you can place two live bamboo stalks in a single vase to represent steady growth in your relationship.

3

FENG SHUI COLORS

"How does color influence our life-world?
First, color defines for us what exists
and what does not exist.
Second, color discloses the status
of one's health and fortunes…
Third, color inspires emotion."

—HIS HOLINESS MASTER LIN YUN

How to Approach Colors

11

COLORS ARE ONE OF THE BASIC WAYS TO ADJUST YOUR FENG SHUI. Humans rely heavily on visuals to adapt to the world around them; therefore, color has a huge influence on how we relate to our moods, healing, and emotions. Color is light, in varying wavelengths. So why not use color to shift your energy?

In nature, color defines the seasons. Winter is dark and white. In spring things begin to sprout green. Summer is bright and sunny and full of vibrant colors. In the fall, the leaves begin to turn yellow and brown. Colors in our environment also indicate the time of day. At dawn colors are soft and muted, at noon colors are vibrant with the intensity of the sunlight, and colors darken as night approaches.

With colors, we also have our own personal cultural conditioning. Our associations with colors depend a lot on where we live. For example, in China, traditionally white is worn to funerals and black to weddings. In the West, it is the opposite. Colors also stimulate nostalgia. Some colors can resonate with particular memories. Whether a color is related to your memory or your cultural conditioning, pay attention to your reactions to colors. Be sure to explore your personal associations and honor them.

Anjie CHO

Hopeful Greens and Blues

12

GREENS, TEALS, AND BLUES ARE ASSOCIATED WITH HOPE, NEW BEGINNINGS, AND GROWTH, LIKE PLANTS AND THE ELEMENT OF WOOD. These colors are calming and relaxing, and lend to tranquility and healthy supportive energy. These are balancing colors and the colors of nature and plants.

In feng shui, green and blue represent life and renewing energy and activate the area of New Beginnings. These two colors can be extremely restorative. Bright fluorescent colors are more stimulating and refreshing. Green is related to the heart chakra, which is related to emotional healing and empathy.

Greens and blues are great colors to use as wall paint color for most rooms in a home. Soft hues are especially beneficial in the bedroom when one needs rest. Placement of green plants (living or fake) also promotes growth and healing in the home. Jade is a wonderfully healing stone you can use in the New Beginnings area of your bedroom to reinforce self-healing.

Elegant Purples and Violets

13

PURPLE IS AN AUSPICIOUS FENG SHUI COLOR CONNECTED WITH WEALTH AND ABUNDANCE, AND OFTEN ASSOCIATED WITH ELEGANCE AND ROYALTY. Purple is the combination of fiery red and relaxing blue. Therefore, this color can harmonize and create inner balance and peace.

Purple is also the color of the crown chakra, which is related to enlightenment and wisdom. This color can be used to activate the Abundance area of your desk, bedroom, or home to attract more wealth and self-worth in your life.

Amethyst is a beautiful crystal that can be placed in your Abundance area to invite prosperity and nobility into your home. Pale and deep violets can be calming and balancing. Purple flowers or accents may be used in the Abundance area.

Anjie CHO

Earthy Yellows, Oranges, and Browns

14

THE COLORS YELLOW, ORANGE, AND BROWN ARE RADIANT, WARM, AND FREQUENTLY FOUND IN NATURE. They are also the colors of the harvest season, which can symbolize both activity and hibernation.

Deep earthy shades indicate strength and endurance while also being nurturing and tranquil. Pale browns and neutral tones of sand and soil are soothing hues, representing stability and the nurturing of mother earth. Brown can be elegant and also symbolize the quiet steadiness of a tree. For a calm atmosphere, stay on the light end, but away from yellow colors. Flesh tones are appropriate for restful rooms such as the bedroom.

On the other end of the spectrum are the stimulating tones of orange and yellow. Bright yellows and oranges are longer wavelengths and can arouse appetite. The brighter hues may be supportive for the center of the home to activate the Health area of the bagua.

Complementary Whites

WHITE SYMBOLIZES PURITY, HEAVEN, AND SIMPLICITY.

15

White is the absence of all color and can represent a blank slate. In nature we see white in clouds and snow. Clouds refer to the heavens while the winter snow reminds us of stark coldness. White is the ultimate yang, or active, color.

White is great as a base to start with, but it is best to avoid creating rooms that are entirely white. White can be sharp and harsh on the eyes. Imagine walking in a field of snow; it is glaringly blinding and exhausting. Our eyes see white as a brilliant color.

Instead try to use whites to contrast other colors. Off-whites are softer and friendlier. I do recommend a pure white paint color for ceilings in a flat finish, as this reflects the most light into the room, creating the appearance of a larger, brighter, and lighter space.

Anjie CHO

Supportive and Neutral Grays

16

GRAYS ARE CONSIDERED TRANQUIL AND QUIET, AS THEY ARE A BALANCE OF BLACK AND WHITE, YIN AND YANG. They are also neutral shades that can complement almost any color. Gray can feel a bit cold, depressing, and isolating, reminiscent of being stuck inside on a rainy day. Gray is thought of as an ambiguous color, as in the "gray area."

Because it is such a noncommittal color, grayish hues are suitable for most spaces. Simply use them in combination with any other color to generate a more sophisticated and supported look.

Gray is also related to the area of Benefactors, which attracts helpful people. In addition, grays are helpful in supporting the intention of the other colors you use in a particular space.

Deep and Dark Blues

DARK BLUES ARE RELATED TO THE CONTEMPLATIVE

17

KNOWLEDGE AREA OF THE BAGUA. Deep hues of blue create a
meditative feeling of exhaling, which relaxes tensions and refreshes the
body. Blue tones can provide a sense of security and calm.

In nature we see dark blues in the night sky or when peering down into
the deep ocean. Blues give an overall quiet and settling feeling, especially
dark blues.

This color also governs the throat chakra, which is the gateway through
which we communicate and express ourselves. Lapis lazuli is a blue stone
that assists in opening up the throat chakra, and supports self-expression
and growth. A piece of this crystal is especially supportive if placed in the
Knowledge or Completion area of your bedroom or meditation area.

Anjie CHO

Fiery Reds

18

RED IS THE MOST AUSPICIOUS COLOR WHEN IT COMES TO FENG SHUI. It is sensuous, dynamic, and very stimulating. While red is appropriate for many applications, it is not suitable for relaxing environments because it can be very active. Take care to use it in moderation, as a little bit of red can go a long way.

It makes perfect sense that red is also associated with fire, passion, and the Recognition area of the bagua.

If you need some more passion in the bedroom, add some red sheets or a red blanket. Buying some new sexy red underwear will also help. If you are looking for a promotion or some recognition in your career, try placing the Mars yantra in the Recognition area of your home office or desk. This fiery red yantra may adjust lack of passion and fame by adding fire.

Wise Blacks

IN FENG SHUI, BLACK IS RELATED TO WISDOM AND

19

KNOWLEDGE. Black is the combination of all colors. It has depth and symbolizes the incorporation of all things. Black is also the most yin or passive color.

Although black can be contemplative, too much will generate a dark look. Excessive black is not appropriate for home interiors because it will absorb light and feel oppressive and depressing. Instead, blacks can be used as dramatic accent pieces.

Because black absorbs, black tourmaline is excellent for protection from negative energy, including electromagnetic smog. Use four pieces to create a grid under your bed, in your bedroom, or for your entire home. Place one piece in each corner (of the bed, bedroom, or entire home). This generates an energetic grid of security and absorbs most types of harmful energy.

Anjie CHO

Romantic Pinks and "Peach Blossom Luck"

20

PINKS AND PEACH TONES ARE CONNECTED TO THE RELATIONSHIP AREA OF THE FENG SHUI MAP. These colors are feminine, nurturing, romantic, soft, and innocent. Pink is also associated with youthfulness, love, and joy.

Pink and peach colors, especially on painted walls, are incredibly flattering for skin tones. You will be seen through "rose-colored glasses" in a pink setting. The color makes you appear healthier and creates a glow.

In feng shui, peach is a very lucky color for attracting a romantic partner. We call it "peach blossom luck." It is ideal to paint your bedroom peach and wear peach to attract your future mate. After you meet the right person, be sure to change the intention of the paint color to support the new relationship rather than attracting a new one!

4

tips
21
through
26

FIVE
ELEMENT
THEORY

*"When human beings lose their connection to nature,
to heaven and earth, then they do not know
how to nurture their environment or
how to rule their world."*

—CHÖGYAM TRUNGPA

_____

How to Use Five Element Theory

IN FENG SHUI, WE EMPLOY FIVE ELEMENT THEORY, A PHILOSOPHY USED TO DESCRIBE THE CYCLES OF NATURE AND HOW THEY WORK TOGETHER AND SEEK TO ALWAYS BE IN BALANCE. The five elements are earth, water, fire, wood, and metal. Five element theory is also utilized in traditional Chinese medicine, Chinese astrology, and martial arts.

The five elements can be used in a "creation" or "overcoming" sequence to produce or reduce an imbalance of a particular element. For instance, if you need more fire, you can add more wood, which produces fire. Alternatively, if you have too much fire, you might add water, which reduces the flames of a fire.

A great and simple way to create balance and harmony is to include something that represents each of these five elements in your space. You can do this by adding colors, materials, or shapes that correspond to each of the elements as described in the following tips.

Anjie CHO

Earth

22

THE ELEMENT OF EARTH IS RELATED TO EARTHY COLORS LIKE BROWN, ORANGE, OR YELLOW AND THE FENG SHUI BAGUA AREAS OF RELATIONSHIPS, HEALTH, AND KNOWLEDGE. Earth also has the qualities of stability and nourishment, like mother earth. The earth element creates metal, because metal ores come from the earth's core. Earth overcomes water, as the banks of a river control the direction of the flow and because soil can muddy water.

You may have too much earth if you care too much for others without first taking care of yourself. For this imbalance you can add metal, which depletes earth, or wood, which breaks up earth. If you are very self-centered, selfish, and care for no one but yourself, you may have too little earth. For this imbalance you can add earth or fire, which produces earth. When earth is balanced you take care of yourself first, which allows you to truly care for others.

Some examples of earth are objects with a square shape; orange, brown, or yellow color; or composition from the earth, such as a large stone sculpture. You can add the earth element with a stone statue or large natural stone such as jasper, which is heavy and from the earth, providing stability and support. A big wood desk is also earth element, as it is brown, earthy in color, squarish and has weight to it.

Water

23

THE ELEMENT OF WATER IS RELATED TO DARK COLORS, LIKE BLACK AND VERY DARK BLUE, AND THE FENG SHUI BAGUA AREA OF PATH IN LIFE. Water has the qualities of fluidity, wisdom, and intelligence. It is also related to your social network and how you interact with the world. The water element creates wood, because water supports plants and trees as well as all life. Water overcomes fire, as it extinguishes the flames.

You may have too much water if you are overwhelmed with social activities and spread yourself too thin. For this imbalance you can add earth, which muddies water, or wood, which depletes water. If you are isolated, with problems connecting with others and opportunities, you may have too little water. For this imbalance you can add water or metal, which generates water. When water is balanced, you connect with the outside world, and it responds to you in a balanced manner where you receive appropriate connections and opportunities.

Water items include wavy shapes and, of course, anything with actual water. A water fountain or fish tank are both simple and beautiful ways to add water to your space. Mirrors support the water element and can visually expand your space. Water represents knowledge and can assist with positive cash flow.

Fire

THE ELEMENT OF FIRE IS RELATED TO THE COLOR RED AND THE FENG SHUI BAGUA AREA OF RECOGNITION. Fire also has the qualities of explosiveness, passion, and sincerity. The fire element creates earth, as ashes transform all back to the earth. Fire overcomes metal, as it causes metal to melt into a liquid.

You may have too much fire if you hold a lot of anger, blow up frequently, and stay angry for long periods of time. For this imbalance you can add earth, which depletes fire, or water, which puts out the flames. If you are fearful of anger and hold it all in, you may have too little fire. When you turn off fire, you also turn off the passion for life. For this imbalance you can add fire or wood, which feeds fire. When fire is balanced, you feel anger when appropriate, recognize and accept it, then let it go.

Fire is red and triangular in shape. In feng shui, fire elements improve passion and recognition. You can add fire to your home with the color red or even with lighting. Lighting and candles also represent fire energy. In some cases when you need to refresh your fire energy, it's a good idea to add a brighter, energy-efficient bulb to an existing light to reinvigorate that fire energy.

Wood

THE ELEMENT OF WOOD IS RELATED TO THE COLORS GREEN AND BLUE AND THE FENG SHUI BAGUA AREAS OF NEW BEGINNINGS AND ABUNDANCE. Wood has the qualities of flexibility, life, and kindness. Wood also symbolizes growth. The wood element creates fire, like the logs in a fireplace. Wood overcomes earth, as the roots of a tree push through and take nourishment from the soil.

You may have too much wood if you are stubborn, inflexible, and un-kind. For this imbalance you can add metal, which chops up wood, or fire, which burns up wood. If you are ungrounded, going this way and that way with the wind, such that you almost don't have a backbone, you may have too little wood. For this imbalance you can add wood or water. When wood is balanced, you are well grounded and stable. You are flexible when you need to be but still hold steadfast to your ideals.

Wood objects to add to your space can be vertical or expansive, such as living plants. Green, living plants also improve the indoor air quality and add life energy to any space. Fake plants work similarly to living plants as long as they are of good quality and look real.

Metal

26

THE ELEMENT OF METAL IS RELATED TO THE METALLIC COLORS, AS WELL AS WHITE AND GRAY, AND THE FENG SHUI BAGUA AREAS OF BENEFACTORS AND COMPLETION.

Metal has the qualities of righteousness, contraction, and joy. The metal element creates water, as drops of water condense on a metal pipe. Metal overcomes wood, such as when an ax chops down a tree.

You may have too much metal if you are rigid and talk excessively without thinking. For this imbalance you can add water, which depletes metal, or fire, which melts and allows metals to be reshaped and refined. If you are unable to speak up for yourself when appropriate you may have a metal deficiency. For this imbalance you can add metal or earth, which produces metal. When metal is balanced, you speak and stand up for yourself and what is right appropriately and with thoughtful certainty.

Metal is associated with circular shapes and the physical element of metal. Metal assists in efficiency and attracting helpful people to your office. Ways to add the metal element to your space include adding metal wind chimes or other natural metal objects. You can find metal Buddhas to balance the five elements in your space as well.

BASIC FENG SHUI PRINCIPLES

*"We shape our buildings,
and afterward
our buildings shape us."*

—WINSTON CHURCHILL

Position Yourself in Command of Your Life

27

IN FENG SHUI WE HAVE A VERY IMPORTANT CONCEPT CALLED THE "COMMANDING POSITION." Ideally, your bed, desk, and stove are positioned so that you can see the door and the expanse of the room, and you have your back against the far wall. You don't want to be directly in front of the door. Instead, across the room, diagonal from the door, is typically the most ideal position.

Where does the idea of the commanding position come from? The feeling of danger and fear is a physiological response that you experience on a subtle level when you cannot see the door or what may be coming your way. Although not everyone is consciously aware of it, it does affect you. It is like water dripping lightly on a stone for years; the stress levels begin to wear you down. Metaphorically, the commanding position places you in command of the room, your home, and your life, because you can see what life brings to you, and you can move forward with your eyes open.

Understandably, this furniture placement may not always be possible, so you can make an adjustment to a potentially unfavorable position by placing a mirror in such a way that you can see the door to the room. Now you're back in command!

The Power of Intention

28

INTENTION IS AN IMPORTANT ASPECT IN FENG SHUI. Remember why you are doing whatever you do, whether you move your bed, add a crystal, or even utter a word. Each action sends vibrations into the universe and can affect you, your home, and even the universe as a whole.

Feng shui depends a lot upon your intention. If you add a green plant for more growth in a specific area of your life, the physical act of placing that object is just one part. The second part is to acknowledge that the placement of that object has created a shift in your energy to set the wheels in motion to achieve your goals.

Let the universe know through action and intention what you truly want, and I promise you will receive something remarkable in return.

SPACE CLEARING

"*Energetically, everything that ever happens*
in a building goes out in ripples like
the effect of a stone being dropped in a pond.
It is recorded in the walls, floor, ceiling, furniture,
and other objects in the place."

—KAREN KINGSTON

———

Re-Dedicate Your Space

29

IN FENG SHUI, THERE IS A LOT OF TALK ABOUT "ENERGY" OR "QI." The qi of a space can influence the present and future circumstances of the inhabitants. Similarly, the "predecessor energy" of a home or object can greatly influence the current qi of a space. This applies to previous owners and residents, vintage furniture, and even used books. Does a place or object hold an imprint of positive, supportive energy? Or does it hold negative and stagnant qi?

Space clearing is an effective way to re-dedicate the invisible energy of a space. It is vital to clear the space of any stale energy and create a clean slate for you and your family. This is especially true if you have a lot of secondhand items.

Remember, once you clear the space or object of the negative energy, replace that energy with positive intention. The following tips offer different ways to clear space, including using orange peels and smudging.

Anjie CHO

Refresh with Orange Peels

30

ON A TYPICAL DAY, I START WITH FIVE DROPS OF ORANGE AND
ONE DROP OF FRANKINCENSE ESSENTIAL OILS IN MY DIFFUSER.
This is my favorite way to clear my work space and begin to create.

In feng shui, oranges and orange peels represent vibrant, life-affirming
yang energy. Yang energy is like the energy at high noon—bright and
strong. Orange essence is refreshing and happy, and contributes positive, fresh,
and brightening energy to our inner and outer environments. Orange essence
will transform an area into a space with vibrant life, giving positive energy.

Fresh orange peels work best because they are the freshest, but you
can also use orange essential oil. Place the orange peel from one orange or
27 drops of the essential oil in a spray bottle and fill it with water. Walk
around your home and spray this citrus essence all around, paying special
attention to dead corners and closets. Orange peel carries vibrant life energy
to clear, and in turn rejuvenate, you and your home. This is excellent to do
on an annual or even monthly basis.

———

Air It Out!

31

A GREAT WAY TO CLEAR YOUR SPACE IS TO USE AN ORANGE-ESSENCE SPRAY IN CONJUNCTION WITH OPENING ALL OF THE EXTERIOR WINDOWS AND DOORS IN YOUR HOME. In BTB feng shui, we have an adjustment for this called "Changing the Qi of the Home."

First, open all of the windows and doors for a minimum of 15 minutes. Allow fresh air to move throughout the entire home. Second, purchase some orange essential oil spray or make your own with water and nine drops of orange essential oil. Shake up the bottle and make nine sprays around the room. Start at the entry door and move around the perimeter of each room in your home in a clockwise fashion. When you end up back at the front door, set your intention that you are filling your home with bright white light and contentment.

It is good practice to clear your space at least once a year. The most auspicious time to do this is on Chinese New Year because the lunar new year is symbolically a great time to clear out the old, stale energy in your home to make space for new, positive energy.

Anjie CHO

Circumambulation and Smudging

32

WHILE WE TRADITIONALLY USE ORANGE ESSENCE IN FENG SHUI FOR SPACE CLEARING, SMUDGING IS ANOTHER METHOD OF CLEARING A SPACE OF NEGATIVE QI. Smudging involves burning sacred herbs and using the smoke to shift energy. It is especially useful on an everyday basis to refresh your home if you've had guests.

In general, the herb is ignited and then gently blown down to an ember to allow for spreading smoke around the room. It is important to guide the smoke to different areas of the room, including corners, inside closets, and in each direction of the compass. Also, be sure to allow the herb to produce enough smoke to fill the air.

The physical movement of walking around the perimeter of a space is described as circumambulating. Typically I recommend starting at the front door (or door to the room) and walking clockwise. Be present and remember to replace the cleared energy with positive intention.

Smudging Herbs

33

WHILE WHITE SAGE IS THE MOST COMMONLY USED SUB-STANCE FOR SMUDGING, IT IS NOT THE ONLY MATERIAL THAT CAN BE USED. Sage is easy to find and is a good general space-clearing material for releasing negative energy.

Native American traditions often include the burning of sweet grass in their clearing rituals. Sweet grass is said to be beneficial in attracting positive spiritual energy and is especially effective in combination with sage.

Tibetans burn juniper in ceremonies to connect heaven, man, and earth. The smell is very strong, and a little goes a long way. Juniper is particularly useful for clearing sacred objects.

Finally, my favorite method of space clearing lately has been smudging with palo santo. As a purifying agent, palo santo wood emits a better smell than sage or juniper when burned. Palo santo can be used as a matter of preference or to avoid allergies. I love its fresh, bright, and minty fragrance.

Regardless of which material you choose, all of these options are time-tested and ancient tools for clearing space and releasing negative energy.

Anjie CHO

A Literal Space Clearing

34

IF YOU LIVE IN A HOME WITH ANY SORT OF HVAC (HEATING, VENTILATION, AND AIR CONDITIONING) UNIT(S), YOU PROBABLY HAVE AN AIR FILTER SOMEWHERE. You might be surprised to find that this filter has a ton of dust and debris that needs some attention. This can literally affect your air quality!

Cleaning HVAC filters and coils helps your appliances run more efficiently because the accumulated debris restricts airflow. When filters and coils are clean, the units use less energy, which saves you money. Some filters can be cleaned and reused, while others may need to be replaced.

In addition, cleaning filters regularly improves the indoor air quality. Filters may harbor bacteria, mold, or allergens. Regularly cleaning filters will minimize any indoor-air-quality issues.

Make Your Heart Sing

35

WHAT MAKES YOUR HEART SING? Did you know that the Recognition area of the feng shui bagua map also governs passion, fire, and the heart? When we sing, we activate fire energy within our hearts. In addition, the area of Completion is related to the mouth and joyfulness.

Take some time every day to sing! Singing not only exercises your lungs and abdominal muscles, it releases endorphins for positive energy. If you're a little shy about it, sing when no one is around. Just sing for yourself. Who cares if your pitch isn't perfect?!

When I sing, I visualize the sound waves twirling through the air toward the other end of the room. This fills the entire room with positive energy and joy. It does not hurt to dance around as well!

ENTRY

"The ache for home lives in all of us,

the safe place where we can go

as we are and not be questioned."

—MAYA ANGELOU

Anjie CHO

Make an Inviting Entry

36

In feng shui, your entry symbolizes opportunities to find you. How will an amazing person or project find you if your door cannot be found? Is it hidden behind bushes or clutter? Is the doorbell broken? Make sure your door is easy to find by painting it red, or even adding plants around the door. Trim overgrown bushes or remove clutter that may be blocking the visibility of your door, and fix the doorbell and buzzer!

Other areas to check include the door number and mat. Is your door number easy to find? Is it clean and secured to the exterior of your home? Is there a clean doormat? Greeting guests with a new doormat invites positive energy.

Remember, not only is your entry the first thing that people see when they visit your home, it is also the first thing that you see when you get home. Make sure it is visible and clean!

Brighten Your Entry

37

THE FIRST THING PEOPLE SEE WHEN THEY VISIT YOUR HOME IS THE ENTRY. What is it that they see? Is the entry well lit? Is it welcoming? Can visitors find the front door easily? The entry and front door of your home represent your face to the world, how the world sees you, and how easily opportunities can come to you.

One way to brighten your entry is literally. Make sure you have a bright and energy-saving light bulb illuminating the entry.

Another option is to hang a feng shui, faceted crystal ball in a dark or small entry. The crystal attracts positive energy, and then disperses it into your home.

In feng shui it is very important to hang crystal balls using a red cord. Red is a very auspicious color and represents protection. It is even better if the cord can be a length that equals a multiple of 9—like 9, 18, or 27 inches. Feng shui crystals are easy to find online, and they come in various sizes. For feng shui purposes, most interior spaces should use crystals of 40mm in diameter or larger.

Anjie CHO

Clean Your Entry

38 THE ENTRY AREA OF YOUR HOME, INCLUDING THE EXTE-
RIOR AND INTERIOR, REPRESENT THE "MOUTH OF QI"—
WHERE ENERGY COMES INTO YOUR HOME. If this area is
congested, cluttered, and in disarray, how can positive energy flow into
your life with ease?

Start cleaning the entry areas of your home. Vacuum your welcome mat,
toss all the clutter that has accumulated over time, and sweep up the dusty
corners. It is important to clean out this area and keep it clean and fresh so
you can attract the best energy in your life.

The door to your living space is something you see every day as you
come home, and it affects you and your mood. A clean and cared-for entry
will give your home and your visitors a sense of place and stability.

Refresh Your Front Door

WALK OUTSIDE TO YOUR FRONT DOOR, AND TAKE A GOOD LOOK AT WHAT YOU SEE. I'm talking about the actual formal entry door to your home.

Make sure to clean your front door of any dirt and dust. Clean around and inside the door jamb and frame, as well as the edges of the door, where dust collects. These areas are often overlooked. Repaint or clean your entry door and make sure that the doorbell, buzzer, and all door hardware are in working condition. Oil any squeaky hinges, and clean or replace the number and name on the door.

Take care to sweep under and vacuum the welcome mat. Because the entry door is your mouth of qi, this is where energy can enter your home. An excellent way to attract more qi is to get a new doormat. Get a new welcome mat, red or black if possible, to attract qi. Ideally, you want to get one that is almost the same width as your front door, or a little larger, not too small. When your entry door stands out, you can differentiate yourself and attract auspicious energy into your home and life.

Anjie CHO

Start Using Your Front Door

40

AS MOST OF US ARE CAR-DEPENDENT, WE OFTEN USE THE GARAGE OR SIDE DOOR AS THE PRIMARY ENTRANCE. It's more convenient and requires less walking.

In feng shui, your formal front door represents the mouth of qi as well as your face to the world. This is how energy, good luck, and opportunities come to you. So if you're not using your front door regularly, that energy has no way of getting into your home and life! Worse, if you keep this important portal closed all the time, you are not able to maximize your opportunities, and you close yourself off from receiving positive energy.

The best way to remedy this situation is simple. Start using your front door again! If possible, open it every day, or at the very least nine times a month. Make an effort to walk around to the front and encourage the beneficial energy to flow and enter your home. If you forget about using it, you miss opportunities to bring positive energy into your life and home.

Add a Fountain

41

A WATER FOUNTAIN IS ONE OF THOSE QUINTESSENTIAL FENG SHUI CURES THAT EVERYONE ASKS ABOUT. Not only does it provide a soothing sound, the moving water can improve your cash flow.

A good location for a fountain would be in the entry of your home, but it is important that the flow of the water is toward your home. For this reason, fountains with a directional water flow are best. It is helpful to have a fountain that you really love and care for. It is also helpful to have all five elements represented in some way.

Water fountains are great ways to add beauty, sound, and humidity for a tranquil and harmonious space. The soothing sounds of trickling water can relax your mind and lower your stress level. The circulating water also releases negative ions, which helps to purify the air. Just like waterfalls and the ocean, the negative ions produced by the circulating water improve mood and induce feelings of well-being. The water also creates humidity that moistens the air for humans and for plants. A fountain is a natural humidifier!

LIVING ROOM

*"There are a thousand little things
we can do to our home that will bring
a sense of dignity to where we spend our time."*

—LODRO RINZLER

Anjie CHO

A Space to Live and Entertain

42

THE LIVING ROOM IS A SPACE TO GATHER, LIVE, AND ENTERTAIN. IN FENG SHUI THIS ROOM IS BEST LOCATED NEAR THE FRONT OF THE HOME. After the foyer, the living room is the most ideal room to encounter as you enter your home. This living room position allows an individual to immediately decompress and relax into the space.

Spend some time arranging your furniture so that most of it is in the commanding position. For instance, it is welcoming and pleasant to face the front of the sofa when you walk in rather than see the back of it.

With the trend in open home plans, it is great to have the spaciousness and integration of eating and cooking, but I find that we still seek intimate areas within the openness. Therefore, take some time to make a variety of spaces in your living room that support different experiences, such as a pair of matching chairs to encourage a one-on-one conversation, or a quiet window seat for reading.

Fish Tanks

IN ASIAN MYTHOLOGY, THERE IS A STORY OF A GOLDFISH, OR CARP, THAT TRANSFORMED INTO A DRAGON. Dragons represent luck and power. In turn, goldfish are auspicious. They can be brought into your home to attract success. For a wealth cure, try adopting eight orange goldfish and one black goldfish.

The ideal location of your tank really depends on your floor plan, but as a general rule, for wealth it may be beneficial to place the fish near the front door of your home, especially in the Path in Life (*KAN*) area of the feng shui bagua map.

If there is a water filter on your tank with any sort of waterfall, it is best to position it so the water falls toward the central part of your home. This represents the cash flowing toward you. You can also place a fish tank in the Abundance (*XUN*) area of your living room. My teacher, Steven Post, suggests locating the tank at eye level, so it is easily accessible to view and touch and creates a sense of peace.

43

Anjie CHO

Nine Fresh Oranges

44

IN FENG SHUI, ORANGES AND ORANGE PEELS CONTRIBUTE POSITIVE, FRESH, AND BRIGHTENING ENERGY TO OUR INNER AND OUTER ENVIRONMENTS. Oranges are very auspicious and lucky in Chinese culture. You can always find oranges as decorations at any Chinese festivity. Oranges can transform the home with vibrant life, giving positive energy.

An easy way to incorporate oranges as a home decoration is to get a lovely bowl. A green, black, or white bowl complements the color orange well. Place this bowl in your living room, taking care to keep the fruit fresh and replenished as the oranges start to get too ripe. When they get very ripe, feel free to eat them!

In feng shui a bowl of fresh oranges adds happiness and brightness to any room.

KITCHEN

"*The Chinese character for Qi*

depicts steam rising over rice,

which provides nourishment.

Qi is considered the life breath

that nourishes and vitalizes nature,

being and knowing."

—STEVEN POST

KITCHEN

A Place to Nourish

45

THE KITCHEN IS THE ROOM IN WHICH WE STORE AND COOK THE FOOD THAT NOURISHES US. I like to think of it as a modern hearth, a place where families gather for warmth around the fire. This is especially the case with today's open kitchen plans.

In feng shui it is said that white is the best color for a kitchen, because it represents cleanliness. Similarly to how white is the ideal color for plates to show off the rainbow of colors in foods, white is also a great color for the walls, cabinets, and backsplash tile of a kitchen.

In particular with kitchen cabinets, be aware of upper cabinets and shelves that do not go all the way to the ceiling. The open space between the top of the cabinets and the ceiling is a place where blocked energy can collect, leading to arguments. If this is something you cannot change, you can put plants, lighting, or beautiful objects in this space to keep the energy alive.

Anjie CHO

Deep Clean the Refrigerator

46

THE REFRIGERATOR IS AN IMPORTANT APPLIANCE IN YOUR HOME, AND IT REPRESENTS BOUNDARIES IN LIFE AND HOW YOU NOURISH YOURSELF IN THE WORLD. It's a good idea to have a well-stocked refrigerator—not too full and not too empty. Or, as we say in feng shui, not too yin and not too yang.

Look at this as an opportunity to deep clean and de-clutter. Empty out your refrigerator and remove anything expired, old, and/or spoiled. Spoiled and expired food symbolizes neglect of one's overall health. If possible, compost the organic material, or find a compost drop-off location, and recycle or reuse the glass and plastic containers.

When cleaning the interior of the refrigerator, I prefer to use natural, non-toxic cleaners such as baking soda to scrub and a mixture of vinegar, water, and eucalyptus essential oil to wipe down and disinfect. Open up a new container of baking soda to absorb any odors in your newly organized and clean refrigerator.

I also keep a clear natural crystal quartz in my refrigerator. I program that crystal with the intention to enhance the life energy and nourishment of the food that I will later eat.

Switch to Non-Toxic Cleaning Products

47

THE INDOOR AIR QUALITY OF OUR HOMES IS OFTEN OVER-
LOOKED BUT IS ESSENTIAL FOR HEALTH AND HEALING.
Americans spend over 90 percent of our time indoors! It is time to
eliminate toxic chemicals from your living environment. These chemicals
are absorbed easily through the air and skin, and are extremely dangerous if swallowed.

Non-toxic, green cleaning products are now easy to find at your local
grocery stores. It is also easy to make your own with household items like
vinegar and baking soda.

My favorite DIY recipe is for an all-purpose cleaning solution. You
combine one part white vinegar and three parts water, with nine drops of
essential oil. Eucalyptus and tea tree oil are good options, as they are
naturally anti-bacterial and anti-microbial. Shake up all of the ingredients in
a spray bottle and you've got a homemade, non-toxic cleaner.

Anjie CHO

Start Composting

48

THE BENEFITS OF COMPOSTING ARE NUMEROUS, WHETHER OR NOT YOU GARDEN OR HAVE A YARD. Composting drastically reduces your organic waste from kitchen scraps and organic yard waste, so you save money on your waste bill while reducing greenhouse-gas emissions through proper degradation. Plus, composting recycles nutrition for the soil.

When you compost organic materials, instead of dooming them to landfills or other trash collections, you prevent production of harmful gases like methane and leachate formulation.

If you live in an apartment without outdoor space to compost, search for local compost drop-off sites. Or better yet, you can do your own indoor composting with a red-worm bin. More information is easily available online.

Composting is among the top options for reducing your carbon footprint, thus doing your part to save our planet. From enriching soil without harmful chemicals to reducing a trash collection bill, time spent composting is time well spent.

Switch to Fabric Towels and Napkins

ACCORDING TO THE NATURAL RESOURCES DEFENSE COUNCIL, "IF EVERY HOUSEHOLD IN THE UNITED STATES REPLACED JUST ONE ROLL OF VIRGIN FIBER PAPER TOWELS (70 SHEETS) WITH 100% RECYCLED ONES, WE COULD SAVE 544,000 TREES."

You can save both money and trees by using reusable and washable fabric items in place of disposable paper towels and napkins. Microfiber towels are especially good substitutes for paper towels for cleaning glass, electronics, and stainless steel surfaces. Microfiber is super absorbent, lint-free, and leaves no streaks. As for napkins, fabric napkins are much more sophisticated and useful than any paper napkins. I have a set of fancy ones for dinner parties and guests, as well as a stack of nice kitchen tea towels that I use as my "everyday" napkins.

Anjie CHO

Use Your Dishwasher

50

EVERYONE LIKES THIS ONE! One great way to preserve water in your home is to use your dishwasher! Most dishwashers now use less water than washing by hand!

Typical dishwashers use approximately 15 gallons of water per load. The newer ones use less. This equals less than five seconds to wash and dry each dish, and I know it takes longer than five minutes to hand wash a load of dishes. Save the most water by running full loads only!

Be sure to use phosphate-free dishwasher detergent, and turn off the heated dry, if possible, for energy savings and extra green points.

If you don't have a dishwasher, soak your dishes, rather than running the water while washing, to save tremendous amounts of water.

Double Your Burners

YOUR STOVE REPRESENTS YOUR WEALTH AND HOW YOU
NOURISH YOURSELF IN THE WORLD. If you are not able to eat well,
how can you perform your best?

Make sure your stove is in the commanding position. This means that
you can see the main entry of your kitchen while using the stove. If this is
not possible, set up a mirror behind or next to the stove so you can see
the door.

Not only will a mirror bring your stove into command, but the mirror
can also multiply your burners. In feng shui, the more burners you have, the
more possibility for wealth. It's like more irons in the fire! Even if your stove
is in command, you can still set up a mirror that reflects your burners.
The more burners, the more abundance and prosperity for the inhabitants
of the home.

Anjie CHO

Can You See Your Stove from the Front Door?

52

GO TO THE FRONT DOOR OF YOUR HOME. Can you see your stove? In feng shui this is a very dangerous set up, and can contribute to bloodshed in the home.

Because this may be a difficult layout to change without doing renovations, a remedial solution is to put up a wall or some kind of visual separation so the sight line from the front door to the stove is blocked. A piece of furniture or even a drape will work. I have used *norens* (traditional Japanese fabric dividers) in kitchen doorways to adjust this sort of feng shui no-no. Just remember to block the view of the burner!

If that's not possible, as a last resort, you can put a feng shui crystal ball up between the door and the stove to counteract the negative qi.

Reduce Bottled Water Usage

53

CONTRARY TO POPULAR BELIEF, BOTTLED WATER IS "SUBJECT TO LESS RIGOROUS TESTING AND PURITY STANDARDS THAN THOSE WHICH APPLY TO CITY TAP WATER," SAYS THE NATURAL RESOURCES DEFENSE COUNCIL (NRDC). Health-wise, plastics are terrible to drink from. There may be Bisphenol A (BPA) or other toxic chemicals and substances in plastic containers that will affect water quality.

Plastic water bottles are also unhealthy for our environment. They take thousands of years to biodegrade and usually end up in landfills.

Water filters are a good way to reduce your environmental footprint while taking care of your health. They can remove contaminants such as rust, dirt, chlorine, lead, silt, and odors, and help you reduce usage of plastic water bottles.

I use a high-quality water filter and drink tap water whenever possible. I also use reusable glass bottles and a seltzer machine as much as possible at home.

Anjie CHO

Rotate the Use of Your Stove Burners

54

MY FAVORITE BURNER ON MY STOVE IS THE ONE ON THE FRONT RIGHT. Which one is your favorite? In feng shui, your stove represents nourishment, as well as career, fame, and wealth. The stove is a modern hearth, the place in the home that provides warmth, safety, and nourishment. This means it is essential to use your stove every day, even if only to boil water, and to keep it very clean and in working order. All of the burners should work properly, and you should wipe down the stove on a daily basis.

So what does this have to do with your favorite burner? Tomorrow when you go to your stove, try using another burner instead of always going to the same one. Open up some opportunities for yourself for success in career, fame, and wealth. Instead of mindlessly using the same "favorite" burner, intentionally make an effort toward something new every day. Again, use the stove at least once every day.

Go Green on Takeout

55

WHEN WE EAT PREPARED FOOD, NOT ONLY ARE THERE TAKEOUT CONTAINERS, THERE ARE STACKS OF PAPER NAP-KINS AS WELL AS PLASTIC WARE THAT YOU USUALLY DO NOT NEED.

The US population tosses out enough paper and plastic cups, forks, and spoons every year to circle the equator 300 times. Help save millions of tons of paper and plastic each year by simply asking the restaurant to not include paper napkins and plastic ware. In many online ordering systems, there is even a checkbox for eco-friendly ordering!

Anjie CHO

Clearly Mark Your Recycling Bins

56 IT IS COMMON KNOWLEDGE THAT RECYCLING HELPS THE ENVIRONMENT BY DIVERTING WASTE FROM LANDFILLS. Although you may know what type of material goes in each bin, it doesn't mean that the other members of your household (or guests) are familiar with the setup.

It only takes a few moments to clearly mark your recycling bins. First, take note of the separation requirements of your municipal recycling. For instance, I have one bin for paper and another for glass, metals, and rigid plastics, because they need to be separated to be recycled by my city's service. Sometimes you can ruin a whole bag of paper with food!

DINING ROOM

"One cannot think well, love well, sleep well, if one has not dined well."

—VIRGINIA WOOLF

All About the Dining Room

IN GENERAL, THE DINING ROOM IS A PLACE WHERE OUR **57** FAMILIES GATHER NOT ONLY TO NOURISH OUR BODIES BUT ALSO TO CONNECT WITH EACH OTHER.

The best dining tables have rounded corners, such as oval or circular tables. A round table symbolizes equality and balance. Rectangular and square tables are okay as long as the corners are not too sharp. Be sure there are enough chairs for each person in the household. This allows every inhabitant to feel acknowledged and nurtured.

Finally, be sure the room is well lit and cared for. If possible, there should be no televisions (which encourage mindless eating), and the décor should feature yang colors that help digestion. Light and bright colors such as blue, green, red, and pink are appetizing and encourage a positive dining experience.

Anjie CHO

Use Your Dining Table

58

SADLY, NOWADAYS DINING TABLES TEND TO BE USED FOR EVERYTHING BUT DINING. If possible, take some time each day to eat mindfully at your dining table.

The dining table symbolizes a space to nourish and feed the body, especially with family and friends. Using it on a daily basis prevents it from collecting dust and clutter and allows you to take some time to nurture yourself.

Since space is often at a minimum, a dining table often doubles as a daytime desk, or you might not have a dining table at all. If you use your dining table as a desk, be sure to put away your work while you eat. If you don't have a dining table, create a small space somewhere that is dedicated to eating one meal. Perhaps clear off the coffee table, keep the TV off, and find a beautiful placemat and dish to serve yourself your meal of choice.

Fresh Flowers for Joy

59

FRESH FLOWERS CAN BRING IN JOY AND UPLIFT THE QI OF YOUR HOME. I find them particularly amazing when located in the dining room, right on the dining table.

It is always great to bring in local and seasonal flowers if possible. Conventional flowers are factory-grown and flown in refrigerated planes from halfway around the world, which is not exactly environmentally friendly. Often they are sprayed with toxic chemicals and preservatives to make them last longer. It's also great to support local farmers.

Be sure to keep flowers refreshed by replacing the water on a daily basis and removing any dead leaves and flowers.

HOME OFFICE

"*If a cluttered desk is a sign
of a cluttered mind, of what, then,
is an empty desk a sign?*"

—ALBERT EINSTEIN

Create a Separate Space

60

YOUR HOME OFFICE REPRESENTS AN IMPORTANT AREA IN YOUR HOME. In feng shui, this area symbolizes your career, wealth, and how you bring yourself wealth in the world. A few simple changes in your home office will support your career and wealth.

If you are able to, dedicate an entire room to your home office. This is the ideal scenario.

If you do not have enough rooms to dedicate one for your office, do your best to separate your desk within the space it is in. You can do this with a freestanding bookcase or a room divider, or even with a fabric panel or drape. This is especially important in a bedroom or living room, to help you focus while working and disengage when not working. Visual boundaries are very important in keeping your work and play times balanced. At the very least, you can get a beautiful piece of fabric or scarf and cover your desk when office hours are over!

Put Your Desk in Command

61

TAKE A LOOK AT YOUR DESK LOCATION DESK IN RELATION TO THE ROOM'S DOOR. I often see clients with their desks facing the wall, leaving their backs to the door. This is a major feng shui no-no. Ideally, you should position your desk so that you can see the door while not being directly in line with the door.

The most auspicious position for your desk is at a diagonal from the door. The desired orientation, called the commanding position, is when you are facing the door and the expanse of the room. This means that you are in command of your life and your career, and can see what the universe has in store for you. The best opportunities will be available to you, and you will be able to see them coming. This position minimizes stress and allows the best flow of energy while working.

If space is at a premium in your home and you cannot face the door, set up a mirror so that while you are sitting at your desk you can easily see the door in the reflection. Small, concave mirrors found in automobile shops are excellent for this job. And remember to keep a minimum of 36 inches clear behind the desk for your chair. This represents the space for your business to grow.

Anjie CHO

Look at the Clutter on Your Desk

62 TAKE A LOOK AT YOUR DESK CLUTTER TO FOCUS ON ANY PROBLEM AREAS THAT MIGHT BE AFFECTING YOUR CAREER AND WEALTH.

Where does your clutter tend to accumulate on your desk? While sitting at your desk, look at the furthest left corner, the furthest middle/top area, and the furthest right corner of your desk. Is there a place that you always pile up paperwork that you plan to get to "one day"? Is there a stack of magazines you're hoping to go through? Is there a specific area you stash all of the mail you haven't opened yet? Clutter on the top left corner may represent stagnation in your cash flow and money. The middle top symbolizes how people are viewing you, which is your fame and reputation. Maybe you need more visibility and/or recognition. The furthest right corner is the relationship area. This may indicate the need to cultivate new and existing relationships.

What is the clutter, and what does it symbolize to you based on the area of your desk it's in?

Go Paperless!

63

WE RECEIVE PILES OF JUNK SNAIL MAIL EVERY DAY—CREDIT-CARD APPLICATIONS, CATALOGS, BILLS—AND TYPICALLY IT GOES STRAIGHT INTO THE TRASH. Going paperless is a simple, pain-free way to stop these mailbox fillers in their tracks *and* reduce the amount of wasted paper our society creates daily.

First, please recycle whatever junk mail you receive. It is a good idea to shred anything with your name on it, and then recycle the paper material. Check your local recycling guidelines to see just how much of this mail—catalogs, magazines, etc.—is eligible for recycling, and put as much of it as possible through the earth-saving cycle!

Second, take a few minutes to unsubscribe to catalogs and switch to paperless billing. You not only save trees, you help save energy, carbon emissions, paper waste, and water.

Third, thank yourself for reducing the vast amount of annoying ads and attempts to increase your monthly spending that come to your home regularly. And know that you've taken a huge step toward preserving the only earth we have.

Avoid Glass Desktops

YOUR DESK POSITION IS IMPORTANT IN FENG SHUI BE-
CAUSE IT REPRESENTS YOUR CAREER AND PATH IN LIFE

You should also look at what material your desk is made of.

Although glass desktops are attractive, modern, and sleek, in feng shui terms they are not ideal if you want success in your career. The transparency of the top may cause important deals and projects to fall through. The delicate nature of glass also makes it difficult to really pore over your work.

Feng shui recommends getting an opaque and solid desktop to ensure financial stability and success in your work. A brown wooden desk can represent earthy stability in your career. A metal desk may assist those in need of additional focus and help improve precision in your work.

Buy Post-Consumer-Recycled Products

MOST OF US KNOW BY NOW THAT WE NEED TO RECYCLE. We have heard it many times: reduce, reuse, and recycle! Note that "recycle" is last on that list. Post-consumer-recycled content is made at least partially from materials that people put in public or private recycling bins. So this material has gone through the hands of a consumer. A label that simply says "recycled" indicates that the product was likely made from virgin material such as leftover scraps from factories or overproduced items.

Why buy post-consumer-recycled products? The items you recycle through municipal recycling eventually need to be purchased by someone in order to be fully recycled. When people like us purchase post-consumer-recycled products, we create a market demand for post-consumer materials. Sadly, if there's no market for those materials, everything we recycle may just end up in a landfill. For the sake of the environment, a good percentage of the paper and plastics that already exist should be salvaged and reused for post-consumer-recycled products.

Please choose post-consumer-recycled paper and other office supplies whenever possible. By creating a market and demand for post-consumer-recycled products, we can support and grow the infrastructure for green living.

Anjie CHO

What Are You Facing at Your Desk?

66 WHAT ARE YOU FACING WHEN YOU ARE SITTING AT YOUR DESK? In the feng shui world, we encourage you to face into the room, in "command" of your life and career.

If this is not possible, and you must face a wall, there are a few ways to improve this situation. You can put a mirror on the wall in front of your desk. Rather than looking at a wall, which represents a block in your forward movement, the mirror will expand your view and allow you to move ahead in your career.

Often people will orient their desks toward a window and an outdoor view. In my experience, although it's nice to face a view, it's not the best position for someone who wants to advance his or her career. Your energy goes out the window and does not stay with your work. Instead, why not have the window to your side so that you can take in the view when you want a break, but it's not distracting you from achieving your career and wealth goals?

Bring Clarity and Focus to Your Work

MIRRORS ARE USED FREQUENTLY AS FENG SHUI ADJUST-
MENT OBJECTS. They can expand your view, eliminate bad energy, and
add positive energy. In your home office, you can use a mirror to bring
clarity and focus to your work.

Place a 3-inch-diameter, round mirror on the ceiling such that it reflects
down on you. It's best to situate this mirror so that it is right above your head
while you are sitting at your desk. Be sure it is securely fastened to the ceiling
so you feel safe.

The mirror can elevate your qi, providing support for your mental focus
and clarity in all aspects of your career and work life, which will in turn provide
abundance and support.

Anjie CHO

Plant in Prosperity Corner

68 ASIDE FROM PUTTING YOUR DESK IN COMMANDING POSITION, ANOTHER POWERFUL WAY TO ATTRACT ABUNDANCE IN YOUR CAREER AND WORK IS TO ACTIVATE THE ABUNDANCE AREA OF YOUR HOME OFFICE.

Stand in the doorway facing into the room or area that is your home office. The area to the far left back is the Prosperity corner of your office. Alternatively, you can locate the Abundance corner of your desktop. For the desktop, while sitting at your desk, the far left corner is the Abundance area. You can stimulate prosperity by purchasing a new, green plant and placing it in this area. In fact, you can even place a plant in both locations for some extra support.

Plants represent growth and flexibility. They attract life and positivity. If you like lucky bamboo, you can get three stalks in a vase to represent growth in your abundance and wealth.

12

tips
69
through
73

BATHROOM

*"There is no need to go to India
or anywhere else to find peace.
You will find that deep place of silence
right in your room,
your garden or even your bathtub."*

—ELISABETH KÜBLER-ROSS

Bathroom Basics

IN TRADITIONAL FENG SHUI, THE BATHROOM IS A PLACE WHERE WATER IS ALWAYS COMING IN AND OUT OF THE HOME. Because water represents wealth and money flow, the bathroom is often seen as a problematic room.

My teachers have taught one disclaimer: at the time that feng shui was developed, bathrooms in ancient China were much different than how they are today in the West. We see them as a luxurious, spa-like space of relaxation. So, although it is important to look at the bathroom, keep in mind the cultural differences.

In general, take care to keep your toilet seat closed, as well as the bathroom door. This will keep the wealth from flowing away from you. On a practical note, the water in the toilet bowl contributes to the humidity in the room. Where does mold and mildew come from? Humidity and moisture! By keeping your toilet seat closed, you reduce the humidity in the air, thereby creating a cleaner and healthier environment.

Anjie CHO

Turn Off the Water When Brushing Your Teeth

70 WATER IS A PRECIOUS COMMODITY, AND WE NEED TO CONSERVE IT. We use up clean water faster than earth can naturally recycle and purify it. Water conservation is essential to living a healthy, holistic lifestyle.

An easy way to preserve water in your home is to turn off the tap when brushing your teeth. I know this seems like a no-brainer, but not a lot of people do this. Simply turn on the water when you need it rather than letting it run while you are actively brushing your teeth. There is absolutely no reason to have water running straight down the drain.

Remember, leaving the water on for even a minute can mean one or more gallons of clean water down the drain!

Water-Saving Aerator

CONSIDER GETTING A LOW-FLOW AERATOR FOR YOUR BATHROOM FAUCET. Low-flow aerators reduce the amount of water coming out of your faucets but do not reduce the water pressure. Depending on the type of faucet, these can be found at your local hardware store for as little as $2 each.

Average faucets have a water flow of 3 gallons per minute (GPM). You can check on the side of your faucet to confirm; sometimes the GPM is stamped on the metal.

An aerator restricts the amount of water that goes through the faucet and also mixes in tiny bubbles of air (hence, "aerate"), so you won't notice a difference in water pressure. This device simply screws on to the mouth of your faucet for easy installation.

Generally, an aerator that limits the water flow to 2.2 GPM or less is considered low-flow. Aerators advertise their GPM on their sides.

So if you have a 3 GPM faucet, you could reduce your water usage by half simply by installing a 1.5 GPM aerator.

Anjie CHO

Post-Consumer-Recycled Toilet Paper

72

ACCORDING TO THE NATURAL RESOURCES DEFENSE COUNCIL, "IF EVERY HOUSEHOLD IN THE UNITED STATES REPLACED JUST ONE ROLL OF VIRGIN FIBER TOILET PAPER WITH 100% RECYCLED ONES, WE COULD SAVE 423,900 TREES."

So, what can we do? Purchase post-consumer-recycled toilet paper! "Recycled" typically means that the content is made from pre-consumer materials, such as the leftover waste from manufacturing. It's good, but not the same as post-consumer. "Post-consumer recycled" indicates that the recycled portion of the product is from consumer waste, like pizza boxes or other materials that people have bought, used, and then separated for recycling. By purchasing post-consumer content, you divert waste from choking our landfills. Recycling truly makes a difference when consumers purchase products manufactured from recycled content.

If we make an effort to purchase more post-consumer-recycled toilet paper, we in turn create a demand for the recycled paper, which will minimize deforestation for virgin paper materials. And they make soft versions now!

Make Your Own Low-Flow Toilet

73

NO MATTER HOW GOOD YOU ARE, SOMETIMES YOU END UP WITH A PLASTIC WATER BOTTLE. One good use for that plastic bottle is to create a do-it-yourself (DIY) toilet-tank water displacer.

Typically toilets use up to six gallons per flush. Sometimes this information is listed at the base of the toilet behind the seat. Here's how to make a DIY displacer to save some of those gallons. Note that this only works for a toilet with a tank in the back.

Take an old water bottle, fill it with water, and place it in the tank of your toilet. That's it! Congratulations, you have made your own low-flow toilet. The amount of water that is displaced by the water bottle is saved with each flush. Be careful not to add too many water bottles, because displacing too much water may affect the flushing quality and mechanism. Start with one bottle, test it out, and see if you want to add more to save more water.

You can also purchase a water displacer. These are sometimes called "Tank Banks" because they save money! A water displacer can easily be installed in any tank toilet and save gallons a day off your water bill. Water displacers are not recommended for high-efficiency toilets.

13

BEDROOM

"You should regard your home as sacred,
as a golden opportunity to experience nowness.
Appreciating sacredness begins very simply
by taking an interest in all the details of your life."

—CHÖGYAM TRUNGPA

Anjie CHO

Your Bedroom Represents You!

74

DID YOU KNOW YOUR BEDROOM ENVIRONMENT GREATLY INFLUENCES YOUR STRESS LEVELS AND ABILITY TO TRULY REST AND REGENERATE? We spend many passive, yin hours sleeping in this room. In feng shui philosophy, your bedroom represents you. You can use feng shui to create a harmonious space of relaxation and repose.

In order to transform your bedroom into a soothing environment, it is important to relocate any stimulating objects. Books, electronics, and work items are often too energizing and engaging for the bedroom. In general, remove these sorts of items, as they may induce stress when you are trying to rest.

Soft hues of blues and greens are the most relaxing and healing colors for the bedroom because they suggest life. Greens and blues represent tranquility and healthy supportive energy. Think of the colors we often find in nature: big trees, the ocean, and the sky above. Feng shui recommends avoiding too much white, which can be stressful on the eyes (imagine being in a field of snow without sunglasses). Additionally, too much red or yellow is often overstimulating. These colors are better used for accents.

Double Up Your Bedroom Objects

75

WHETHER YOU ARE IN A RELATIONSHIP OR LOOKING FOR A RELATIONSHIP, TAKE A LOOK AROUND YOUR BEDROOM. How many things are in pairs, and how many single objects are there? These objects are metaphors.

Photographs or artwork of a single person, and a single nightstand, count as singles. It is beneficial to have two nightstands, two bedside lamps, couples in photographs or art…do you see a trend? One great way to bring in that relationship energy is to purchase two new lucky bamboo stalks. Make sure they are straight and not the curly type. Straight bamboo represents upward and positive growth of similar and balanced partners. Place the two stalks in a vase with water together. This is about having pairs in unity.

If you are single, this means you are ready for an equal partner in your life and have made space for them. If you are in a relationship, it symbolizes a balanced and supportive relationship.

Anjie CHO

Location, Location, Location!

76

TAKE A LOOK AT WHERE THE BEDROOMS ARE LOCATED IN RELATIONSHIP TO THE ENTRY DOOR OF YOUR ENTIRE HOME.

It is best to locate bedrooms for family members toward the back of the residence. This places the inhabitants in a commanding position of the space. If possible, the parents' room should be the furthest to the rear, because this places them in the most control of the space. If the child's room holds the furthest position from the front door, the child might have power over the parents. Ideally, it should be the reverse, where the parents are in charge.

If a family member has a bedroom very close to the front door, he or she may feel easily divided from the rest of the family and spend less time at home. Guest bedrooms are better suited closer to the entry of the home, so your guests don't stay beyond their welcome.

Twin? Queen? King?

77

YES, THE SIZE OF YOUR BED DOES MATTER! But in this case, bigger is not always better. Twin beds are okay for children. They're even okay to push up against the wall if you have to. But a twin bed is not ideal for an adult that is in or would like to be in a romantic relationship. There is simply no room for anyone in your bed or in your life.

The king-sized bed, including the California king, is like having a vast desert separating you from your partner! Besides placing partners far apart, the box springs required for such large beds come as two separate pieces, creating a divide between the two partners. This is not conducive to a compatible and positive relationship between two partners.

It is better to get a bed that's comfortable but with a single box spring. If that's not possible, you can put a piece of red fabric between the box springs and mattress to energetically repair the divide.

Anjie CHO

A Space for Each Partner

78

IF YOU ARE IN A RELATIONSHIP, AND ESPECIALLY IF YOU ARE LOOKING FOR ONE, THE MOST IDEAL LOCATION FOR YOUR BED IS WITH THE HEAD AGAINST A WALL, AND THE FOOT OF THE BED OPEN TO THE CENTER OF THE ROOM WITH SPACE ON THE LEFT AND RIGHT SIDES. In other words, it is ideal to set up the bed so that there is clear and balanced open space on both sides.

There are two feng shui implications of having one side of the bed next to the wall. First, your qi will be unbalanced. It will be weaker on the side next to the wall, whether the weakness affects one side of your body or the person sleeping on the wall side. Second, if you are looking for a partner, by pushing the bed against the wall, you're not allowing space for someone to come into your life. If you are in a relationship, one person is more crammed in, which may represent an unbalanced dynamic in the relationship. One partner may feel more locked in or controlled. If the left or right side of your bed is pushed against a wall, this sends the universe the message that the balance of energy between you and your partner is not equal.

Update Your Bed Linens Based on Your Mood

79

SINCE YOU SPEND MANY PASSIVE YIN HOURS ASLEEP IN BED, THE COLOR OF YOUR BED LINENS CAN GREATLY AFFECT YOUR MOOD AND ASSIST IN MANIFESTING CHANGE.

Although I like white linens, they are generally viewed as too metal, meaning too stark or harsh for a bedroom. If you love white like me, go for a soft ivory, or mix it up with some accent colors in your pillows or a throw.

If you're looking to spice things up, deep reds and eggplant purples are both great colors to invoke passion. Yellow is earthy and good for those who need more stability or support. Greens and blues are healing and relaxing colors. They may be helpful if you have trouble sleeping and getting fully rested, while pink or peach is excellent for attracting a partner.

Anjie CHO

Headboard for Stability

80

I FIND THAT A LOT OF PEOPLE DON'T HAVE HEADBOARDS FOR THEIR BEDS. Headboards are so important for relationships in feng shui, because they represent stability and connectedness in a romantic relationship. Do you have a headboard? If not, maybe it's time to get one.

A solid and sturdy headboard is like a strong backbone for a relationship. Be sure the headboard is fastened securely to the bed, rather than attached to or casually leaning against the wall. When the headboard is not securely attached to the mattress, the stability that the headboard can provide is compromised.

In selecting the best feng shui headboard, choose something solid. A solid and stable headboard without major perforations is preferred. The shape is also important. Rectangular, rounded, and heart-shaped are all acceptable. Avoid bars or anything with many perforations, as that can feel like imprisonment or instability. There is not a huge difference between a solid wood and a soft upholstered headboard, as long as both partners are comfortable with the style. Remember, it is there to support both of you!

Art in the Bedroom

81

TAKE SOME TIME AND LOOK AT WHAT YOUR BEDROOM ARTWORK SYMBOLIZES. The bedroom is a place of rest and relaxation. Any artwork that is tranquil and nurturing in color and subject matter is ideal, especially if you have trouble sleeping. Pale, muted, or dark blues, greens, pinks, and purples in art can create a restful mood in a bedroom. If you want to bring in a little more spice and passion, add red artwork to bring in some fire energy.

As far as imagery, feng shui encourages you to have things in pairs in the bedroom. Pairs of images, whether they show people or objects that are similar but not necessarily identical, give the universe the message that you are open to or are currently in a partnership that is balanced and equal with another person. I'm not just talking about images of couples, but perhaps two similar pieces of art in similar frames. Opt for images of loving couples or things in pairs.

Finally, are family photos or photos of Mom and Dad facing the bed? How unsexy is it to have Mom, Dad, and/or a sister staring at you while you're getting romantic? A photo of you and your partner is okay. If possible, place family photos in another part of your home.

Anjie CHO

What's Underneath?

82 WHAT IS UNDERNEATH YOUR BED INFLUENCES YOUR SLEEP AND WELL-BEING. Our beds and bedrooms are tied closely to our personal energy, because we spend a lot of passive time in the bedroom sleeping, but we often forget to look underneath the bed.

It is recommended that you keep nothing under your bed so that the energy and qi can flow easily around you while you sleep. We spend many idle hours asleep, and during this time we are susceptible to the energies of any objects beneath the bed. Clutter under the bed may symbolize unacknowledged blocks in your personal life and relationships. Therefore, what we sleep above affects us!

If you must have storage under your bed, stick with soft, bed-related items such as linens, blankets, and pillows. Be sure to stay away from sharp objects and specifically anything negatively nostalgic, like photos of ex-partners.

A Pair of Nightstands

83

IN FENG SHUI, IT IS VERY IMPORTANT TO HAVE SPACE ON BOTH SIDES OF YOUR BED, WITH A NIGHTSTAND ON EACH SIDE, TO SUPPORT AN EXISTING OR PROSPECTIVE ROMANTIC RELATIONSHIP. This is a way to let the universe know you have made a special space for an equal partner in your life.

The nightstands need not match exactly, but it is best when they are similar in dimension. Avoid extreme differences in size, which may indicate an imbalance in the relationship. If one nightstand is much more spacious and takes up more space, that may indicate an unbalanced power dynamic between the partners.

It is also a good idea to have a lamp for each partner. If you are looking to meet someone, the lamp adds fire energy. The fire calls attention to the space you have made available for your future partner.

Anjie CHO

What Is on the Other Side of Your Head?

84 WHEN LOCATING YOUR BED, TRY NOT TO PLACE THE HEAD OF YOUR BED ON A WALL WITH A TOILET OR STOVE ON THE OPPOSITE SIDE. This can cause a lot of problems for the person sleeping in that bed, including headaches and other health problems.

It's best to move the bed. If that's not possible, place a mirror on the wall over the bed to insulate the person from the flushing water energy of the toilet, or the heat and fire of the stove.

tips
85
through
87

MEDITATION
SPACE

*"Happiness is when what you think,
what you say, and what you do are in harmony."*

—MAHATMA GANDHI

MEDITATION SPACE

Define Your Space

108 WAYS
TO CREATE
HOLISTIC
SPACES

85

FENG SHUI IS A PHILOSOPHY DEVELOPED IN ANCIENT CHINA THAT OUTLINES POSITIVE WAYS IN WHICH TO ORGANIZE YOURSELF IN YOUR ENVIRONMENT. Meditation is a practice in which you can learn to become familiar with your inner landscape. Both feng shui and meditation are used to generate harmony and peace within your life. Why not use feng shui to create a sacred space in which to meditate that can support and improve your meditation practice?

Select a dedicated space that you can routinely go back to for your meditation practice. It can be the corner of your bed, a room in your home, or a place outside in your backyard. My meditation space is a quiet section of my living room that faces a river view. It is okay if you cannot find a perfectly quiet spot. Life is full of distraction, and part of meditation is to learn to accept the interruptions.

You can further differentiate your space by sitting on a special pillow, cushion, or blanket. I have a couple of buckwheat zafu cushions specifically designed for meditation. This can help you to dedicate and define your special spot.

131

Anjie CHO

Dedicate and Clear the Space

86

AFTER YOU HAVE SELECTED YOUR MEDITATION SPACE AND DEFINED IT PHYSICALLY, IT IS OF UTTER IMPORTANCE TO CLEAR AND DEDICATE THE AREA ENERGETICALLY. Space clearing dedicates the invisible energy of the space so you can start fresh and set your intention for the space, the particular moment, and your life.

In feng shui, oranges and orange peels represent vibrant, life-affirming energy. Orange essence is refreshing, happy, and contributes positive, fresh, and brightening energy to our inner and outer environments. You can use nine drops of orange essential oil in an aromatherapy diffuser to transform your area into a space with vibrant, life-giving, positive energy. Remember, when you clear the space of the existing energy, be sure to replace it with positive intention.

Add a Crystal for Clarity

87

FENG SHUI CRYSTALS ARE USED TO ADJUST THE FLOW OF ENERGY IN A SPACE. They are particularly effective for bringing light, brilliance, and clarity to your meditation practice. Feng shui crystal balls are made of faceted, leaded glass.

For this application, purchase a crystal that is a minimum of 40mm in circumference and place it in the center of your meditation space, above your head where you're sitting, or just in front of you so you can see it. The ball should be hung with a red string in a length that is a multiple of 9, for example 18, 27, or 36 inches.

Use this feng shui faceted crystal to create your own sacred meditation place and to create harmony and peace in your inner and outer spaces.

CLOSETS

"The home should be the treasure chest of living."

—LE CORBUSIER

Closet Symbolism

88 TAKE A LOOK AT WHERE YOUR CLOSETS ARE LOCATED BASED ON THE BAGUA MAP. Take special note of which closets are cluttered or unused. Maybe you are afraid to open one of the closets because you need to go through it! These can represent hidden or unacknowledged issues.

For instance, an unused closet in Benefactors may represent helpful people that you have had in your life all along but have not yet tapped into or recognized. You just need to look and ask them for support. A cluttered closet in Abundance may indicate that your wealth is tied up or buried under personal issues or blocks.

If you have a closet in the feng shui area of Path in Life, maybe there's a path you have not yet seen. Are you open to seeing an alternate direction with your career? Or what about a closet in Relationships? Perhaps that relationship you want has been hard to find or hidden. Maybe you need to look a little deeper and open the door to a partner who was always there. And if you have a cluttered closet in Relationships, maybe it's time to de-clutter things and make some space for the love in your life.

Create a Space in Your Closet

89

FENG SHUI PRINCIPLES ENCOURAGE US TO PEEK INTO THOSE DARK CLOSETS, OPEN UP ALL THE WINDOWS, AND REALLY START SHIFTING THE ENERGY IN OUR SPACES. In feng shui, we seek to release stale, stuck energy and welcome in new, vibrant life energy.

Set aside a box for items that have not been worn in the last three years. If there are things that are in poor condition, you can donate those items to textile recycling. There are organizations that collect usable, as well as unusable, clothing and shoes. The unusable shoes and textiles can be made into rags or shredded and recycled for other uses.

Keep in mind that in feng shui, if your closet is full, you will have room for nothing new. This applies literally and metaphorically. If your closet is full, you will have no space to accept new opportunities. There is no room to grow. So, recycle anything that you don't need, and create a vacuum for the universe to bring something new and fantastic into your life.

PLANTS

*"Working with plants, trees, fences,
and walls, if they practice sincerely
they will attain enlightenment."*

—DŌGEN

Add Houseplants

90

DID YOU KNOW THAT HOUSEPLANTS IMPROVE THE OVERALL INDOOR AIR QUALITY IN YOUR HOME? While it's a well-known fact that plants convert carbon dioxide into oxygen through photosynthesis, many houseplants also remove harmful chemicals such as trichloroethylene, benzene, and formaldehyde from the air. They also add natural beauty to your home, bringing some nature inside.

From the feng shui perspective, plants add the wood element: life energy and flexibility for the inhabitants of the home. They can create a softer and more vibrant energy in a home and are healing visually and physically.

The areca palm, mother-in-law's tongue, and the money plant all promote blood oxygenation; reduce eye, respiratory, and headache irritation; increase human productivity; reduce energy costs; and add life energy.

Lucky Bamboo

BAMBOO IS A PLANT THAT IS ABUNDANT IN ASIA AND GROWS VERY QUICKLY. In feng shui, it represents upright and honest growth as well as flexibility and adaptability. The bamboo plant does not flower or fruit—its lifespan is long but simple. It is also hollow, which represents an empty heart of humbleness. Coincidentally, in western culture it is a symbol for the green (sustainability) movement.

In feng shui, bamboo is best when it is straight and not curly or twisted, which can represent the opposite of upright and positive growth. Bamboo represents the wood element of kindness, flexibility, and healing growth. Plants also add life energy to a space. Bamboo is great because it can thrive in a variety of lighting conditions, in water or in soil, and it's very easy to find.

If you're looking for more prosperity, you can place three or nine stalks in the Abundance area of your home, office, or bedroom—better yet, in all three locations. The bamboo will represent positive and steady growth.

Anjie CHO

What to Look for in Houseplants

92

INDOOR TREES AND PLANTS PROVIDE POSITIVE LIFE ENERGY FOR HOME QI. But some types of plants are better than others.

As a rule of (green!) thumb, in feng shui we generally prefer plants with soft and rounded leaves. This shape offers a softer and gentler energy. Plants with sharp leaves, thorns, or spiky needles are best avoided for feng shui applications. If you have these in your home already, it's okay to keep them as long as they are healthy and well taken care of. For example, maybe you have a great attachment to a cactus that you received from your grandmother years ago. This is fine, but in general, if you want to add a plant to your home with a feng shui intention, go for something less prickly.

Always be sure to research the right plants for the type of daylight available in your selected space. A plant that is not suited for your indoor space will be challenging to care for and will not thrive, and that's just not good feng shui.

Fertilize with Organic Compost

93

COMPOSTING IS NATURE'S WAY OF RECYCLING TO REDUCE WASTE AND ENSURE THAT ORGANIC MATERIALS ARE RETURNED TO THE EARTH. Produced using scraps from already-eaten food and other organic waste, compost is natural fertilizer, balances pH, and improves soil content with nutrients that are vital for the growth of many plants, from food plants to pretty plants.

Chemical fertilizers often leave behind a wealth of heavy metals (such as lead, arsenic, and cadmium) that can build up over time. Overuse of chemical fertilizers can actually bring death to the soil, making it dependent on these same fertilizers, thus costing even more money over time. Composting skirts this issue entirely, as compost is composed only of organic materials.

Whether you use your own or purchase some from a local source, organic compost is a holistic way to "feed" your plants. Your plants will thrive and flourish!

Anjie CHO

No More Dried Flowers

94 WHEN I WAS GROWING UP I USED TO DRY FLOWERS AND USE THEM AS DECORATION IN MY HOME. Little did I know that in feng shui, dead flowers bring dead energy into a home. While fresh flowers symbolize joy and life energy, dried flowers represent the opposite: sadness and death.

If possible, it's best to toss them into the compost bin. I love how composting organic material can transform waste into something productive.

Some of my clients have sentimental dried flowers, such as their wedding bouquets. As long as this does not have negative emotions attached to it, such as might come with a divorce, you can clear the bouquet as you would a secondhand object, and keep it! Place 27 drops of orange essential oil in a spray bottle and fill it with water. Spray this essence on the dried flowers to clear away old energy and rejuvenate them with vibrant new energy.

DOORS AND WINDOWS

"Be an opener of doors."

—RALPH WALDO EMERSON

All About Doors and Windows

IN FENG SHUI, DOORS REPRESENT THE MOUTH, AND WINDOWS REPRESENT THE EYES, OF THE INHABITANTS IN A HOME.

95

If you have squeaky, stuck, or otherwise problematic doors, this may represent challenges in communication. This is especially true for the entry door, as it sets the mood for your experience of your home. If you have a squeaky, "crying" door, it sets the tone for negativity every time you walk into your home. Get out the toolbox and oil any squeaky hinges, and repair any problematic doors.

In feng shui, windows represent the eyes of the people of the home. Therefore, windows should be kept in good repair and operable. Windows should be clear and easy to open, so you can feel seen and heard as well as nourished.

Finally, make sure that all doors can open fully to 90 degrees. That means no clutter behind the doors. Doors govern how qi comes into your space. If your doors cannot open fully, you're cutting off the amount of energy that could enter your space.

96   WINDOWS ARE THE EYES OF YOUR SPACE. Make sure yours are clean!

Dirty and dusty windows can affect your ability to see and communicate with the world and represent a lack of clarity in your life. Take special care to wash them well inside and out, and make sure the frames are in good repair so you can open and close them easily. Your environment and your perspective become clearer, brighter, and more vibrant when you clean your windows.

Instead of a toxic commercial glass cleaner, try a green option or make your own using one part vinegar for one part water, and substitute newsprint for paper towels.

Improve your outlook by maintaining clean windows. Trust me; it makes a huge impact and allows you to see your world with more clarity.

Where Are Your Secondary Doors Located?

97

A SECONDARY DOOR MAY BE A BACK OR SIDE DOOR THAT OPENS TO THE EXTERIOR AND IS USED AS AN ALTERNATIVE ENTRY, SUCH AS THE GARAGE DOOR OR SIDE DOOR. These secondary doors, depending on the location, may be positive or negative and are definitely something to pay attention to.

The best location for a secondary door is in Benefactors, because it may indicate additional helpful people to support you in your life.

Locations to be concerned about would be in Relationships, where it may mean that there are extra marital partners or affairs in a relationship. Also watch out for a back door in Abundance or Recognition. Your wealth or fame may leak out this additional door. In both of these situations, the most ideal adjustment is to place a bell or chime on this door. The bell or chime symbolizes an alarm that will sound to alert the members of the household of any danger.

Anjie CHO

Piercing Heart Doors

98

IN FENG SHUI, IT IS IMPORTANT TO WATCH OUT FOR THREE OR MORE DOORWAYS IN A ROW. This is called "piercing heart doors." Open doorways without a door are also included in this definition of "doorway."

We need to watch out for this issue, because it can cause heart-related problems, physically and metaphorically. There is a feeling of contraction then openness, contraction then openness, and contraction and openness again. The feng shui remedy for this is to hang a feng shui faceted crystal ball from the ceiling between each doorway. For instance, if there are three doorways, you would hang two crystals total (one between each pair of doorways). If there were four doors in a row, there would be three crystals. Each crystal must be strung on a red string long enough that the crystal aligns with the top of each door header, without hitting the door when it swings out.

Use a feng shui crystal that is a minimum of 40mm in diameter. Since the crystals are multifaceted, just like with sunlight, they take the harmful energy and disperse it so that it is more gentle on your life and the energy of your home.

THE HOLISTIC HOME

"You may live in a dirt hut with
no floor and only one window,
but if you regard that space as sacred,
if you care for it with your heart and mind,
then it will be a palace."

—CHÖGYAM TRUNGPA

Nine Minutes a Day Keeps the Feng Shui Master Away!

99

PRETTY MUCH EVERYONE IN THE WESTERN WORLD HAS CLUTTER. WE HAVE A LOT OF "STUFF." Stuff is a modern-day problem. It is not necessarily bad or good, but it may represent and cause blocks or stuck energy in your home and your life. That pile of magazines collecting dust in the living room may not only be an eyesore but also a constant reminder of another thing to clean. Or another item on the to-do list. Or even a source of guilt. It takes a lot of energy to ignore that clutter!

Please do not be too hard on yourself if you do have clutter; take it step by step. Start with the easy items that you know you no longer want. I suggest you start with nine minutes a day. Set an egg timer, and just do nine minutes of clutter clearing, then feel good about it!

To be clear, clutter is not always negative. It is okay as long as it doesn't hinder your life or cause guilt and distress. But it may be a problem if it prevents you from achieving your goals and leaves you feeling stuck.

Anjie CHO

Eliminate EMFs

100 IN THE MODERN WORLD, WE ARE INUNDATED BY DANGER-
OUS ELECTROMAGNETIC FIELDS (EMFS) AND RADIATION
EMITTED BY ELECTRONIC DEVICES SUCH AS WI-FI, MOBILE
PHONES, COMPUTERS, AND EVEN THE ELECTRICAL WIRING
IN OUR HOMES. EMFs produce stress on the body and cause health
problems such as fatigue, headaches, and even nausea.

If possible, I encourage you to reduce the number of electronic devices
in your home. An easy place to start is in the bedroom, where EMFs affect
you during passive sleep time. Simply unplug or remove unnecessary
devices. It is recommended that any electronics (including extension cords
and any other cords or charging devices) remain a minimum of five feet away
from where you sleep. Battery-operated devices are okay.

A secondary benefit is that you will reduce your energy use and costs,
making your home not only more healthy, but also greener.

Switch to a Green Energy Provider

101

AN EASY WAY TO MINIMIZE YOUR CARBON FOOTPRINT IS TO SWITCH TO A RENEWABLE ENERGY PROVIDER. Switching to green power does not typically mean that you need to install solar panels or a windmill on your roof. Although that is sometimes an option, in most urban areas you can simply call your electricity provider and request to be switched to a green or renewable energy source. You may see a small increase in your monthly bill, but in my experience it is very minimal.

Signing up for renewable energy will help your home substantially reduce its carbon footprint through the use of wind, solar power, or other renewable sources. If applicable in your state, your energy company will still deliver your electricity, but they will buy your power from a company that creates energy sustainably. You can also look into Renewable Energy Certificates (RECs) to offset your "dirty" electricity usage.

Anjie CHO

Repair or Toss Anything Broken

102

YOU KNOW THAT OLD LAMP YOU HAVE BEEN MEANING TO FIX? BROKEN THINGS MAY REPRESENT WEAKENED ENERGY. They can also be a guilty and constant reminder of something that you "should" do.

A broken doorbell may be hindering your chances of getting a new job or meeting a new person. A stove in disrepair may represent a block in your wealth and nourishment. Even that burned-out light bulb in your desk lamp needs to be replaced. It may prevent you from coming up with some bright ideas in your career.

What's stopping you from repairing that object? If it is important to you, get it repaired, or give it away to someone who can. Don't let that stuck energy stop you from moving forward in life.

Turn Off Unnecessary Lights and Electrical Devices

CONSIDER TURNING OFF SOME LIGHTS IN YOUR HOME **103** DURING THE DAY OR ALTOGETHER TO SAVE ENERGY. An easy way to incorporate this is to upgrade to a light switch with an occupancy sensor. That means that when you leave the room, the light will turn off automatically. This can be effective in areas like basements and bathrooms.

Use natural daylight, which is better for your mood, for the earth, and for your budget! Even if you leave the room for only a few minutes, you save energy and money by turning off the lights.

Anjie CHO

Mirrors in the Home

104 MIRRORS ARE USED FREQUENTLY AS FENG SHUI ADJUST-
MENT OBJECTS TO TWEAK SITUATIONS THAT ARE LESS
THAN IDEAL. Mirrors can add water energy, expand your view, eliminate
negative energy, and add positive qi. They are often used to adjust your
view and put you back in the commanding position.

Mirrors are particularly useful for any weak or missing areas of the feng
shui bagua map. If you lay the bagua map on your space and there is a missing or weak area, placing a mirror facing into your home (with the back facing
the missing or weak area) will help to expand and take back some of that
area. Mirrors can also be used to make up for any missing area.

Be sure the mirrors are not broken or jagged. Mosaic mirrors or mirrors
that are divided up are not appropriate for feng shui applications because
they promote disjointed energy.

Plug Into Power Strips

USE POWER STRIPS, AND TURN THEM OFF WHEN NOT IN USE. **105**
You can purchase power strips at any hardware store for around $10.

A lot of electronics, especially those with any sort of standby light, continue to draw energy although they appear to be off. This is called "vampire power." On average, 40 percent of electricity used to power home electronics is consumed while the products are turned off but still plugged in. When plugged in but not on, all appliances draw a phantom load equal to 30 percent of their full load.

If you plug electronics into a power strip and then turn off the strip when you are not using them, you can ensure they will no longer draw small amounts of electricity when turned off. This may be helpful for appliances, printers, DVD players, and other peripheral devices, including televisions and gaming systems.

Important note: Turn off your power strips when you leave for significant energy savings.

Anjie CHO

Healthy Paint

106

THE SIMPLEST WAY TO REDEFINE AN AREA IS WITH PAINT COLORS. This is a fairly easy and inexpensive way to change up the way your home looks and feels. But no matter what color you choose, the type of paint you use can make a difference.

The green option is a low- or zero-VOC paint. VOC stands for volatile organic compounds. VOCs are chemicals added to paint for a variety of reasons, including color enhancement, increased adhesiveness, and increased ease of spreading. Despite these conveniences, VOCs are extremely dangerous to humans, and the use of them in many paints results in indoor air being anywhere from three to five times more polluted and harmful than outdoor air. Traditional paints have VOCs, which release toxins into the air for years after the paint is applied. In no way is that good for anyone in your home.

Today, many paint companies offer low- or zero-VOC options. In addition to the long-term benefits in terms of air quality, they have minimal odor when wet! There are even zero-VOC food-based paints made with milk casein.

Uplift Your Home with Artwork

ARTWORK IS A GREAT, HOLISTIC WAY TO UPLIFT THE **107**
ENERGY OF YOUR HOME. Art can bring in beauty as well as positive qi.

First of all, we can look at subject matter. Choosing artwork is really a matter of personal preference, but something optimistic and uplifting is generally more positive than something dark and depressing. That said, go with what makes you feel good inside.

Also, look at where the art came from. You might have pieces that have been passed down to you. What is the predecessor energy attached to the art? Is it helpful or harmful to you? If necessary, do some energy clearings to really make the art your own.

Finally, make sure the height of the artwork is appropriate for the area it is in. While it depends on the situation, a good rule of thumb is for the art-work to be at a standing person's eye level or higher. Artwork that is too low may bring down your energy levels.

Anjie CHO

Love Your Home!

108

HERE WE ARE AT NUMBER 108, MY FINAL TIP TO CREATE HOLISTIC SPACES!

You have learned 107 ways to create holistic spaces that support and nurture you and your loved ones. As you incorporate these tips into your home, remember: It is your home, so your energy, and your intentions, are key.

Each time you try a feng shui adjustment, pay attention to how it feels to *you*. Does the shape or color or object placement feel good to you? If not, try a few subtle shifts until it does.

You want to look around your space and love the way it looks and feels. The more you do, the more these adjustments, and your home as a whole, will serve you.

Whatever you desire for your space and your life, bring love and intention to it. When you love your home, you will truly be living in a holistic space that supports and nurtures you and your loved ones.

"Om mani padme hum—the jewel is in the lotus."
—Sanskrit mantra

RESOURCES

RESOURCES

For more information please visit these websites:

ANJIE CHO

Anjie Cho Architect PLLC

www.anjiecho.com

HOLISTIC SPACES

Anjie's online blog and store

www.holisticspaces.com

GEOMANCY/FENG SHUI EDUCATION ORGANIZATION

www.geofengshui.com

BTB FENG SHUI™ MASTERS TRAINING PROGRAM

www.btbmastersfengshui.com

SHAMBHALA MEDITATION

www.shambhalaonline.org

ABOUT THE AUTHOR

ANJIE CHO IS A REGISTERED ARCHITECT AND FENG SHUI INTERIOR DESIGNER. Since 1999, she has been creating beautiful and nourishing environments. A graduate in Architecture from the College of Environmental Design at the University of California at Berkeley, Anjie is a sought-after expert in the fields of feng shui and green design.

Anjie is also the founder of HOLISTIC SPACES, a blog and online store that integrates beauty, spirituality, and green design. Anjie is a LEED Accredited Professional and certified feng shui consultant from the BTB Feng Shui Masters Training Program. She lives in the Lower East Side of New York City with her husband and her Chihuahua, Javier.

66895305R00095

Made in the USA
Lexington, KY
27 August 2017